The Savvy Career Counselor:

Coaching Career Clients On Salary and Other Workplace Negotiations

By Karen James Chopra, LPC, MCC, NCC

The Savvy Career Counselor: Coaching Career Clients On Salary and Other Workplace Negotiations

Copyright 2012 by Karen James Chopra, LPC, MCC, NCC

All rights reserved. No part of this book may be reproduced in any form or by any electronic or mechanical means including information storage and retrieval systems without permission in writing from the author, except by a reviewer who may quote brief passages in a review.

Library of Congress Cataloging-in publication data

ISBN: 978-0615607726

I. Negotiating II. Career Advice III. Workplace skills—negotiating IV. Career coaching

HD58.6.c39 2012
658.4 ch

A Note on Integrative Career Counseling and The Savvy Career Counselor Series

Integrative Career Counseling (ICC) is a framework that I have developed to work effectively with career clients regardless of the other issues that may be present in their lives, including mental illness--such as depression, anxiety and bipolar disorder; family stress, such as divorce, addiction, job loss; and persistent self-defeating patterns—from workaholism to low-self esteem. You can find more information on my website: www.ChopraCareers.com/integrative-career-counseling, and sign-up to receive emails about the ICC model and upcoming trainings.

ICC is premised on the idea that all but those clients in the most acute stages of a crisis are able and entitled to pursue their career goals and dreams. In order to support clients, mental health counseling theories and techniques are integrated into the career counseling process to provide a seamless intervention that supports a client's career work.

The ICC model addresses four levels of client needs. Counselors move among the levels of the ICC model in response to what the client needs in that moment. The model ensures that clients don't get "stuck", because there is always a client need that can be attended to in the session. The model also ensures that career work remains the guiding focus of counseling—mental health counseling is incorporated only as far as is needed to achieve the client's career goals.

The Integrative Career Counseling Model

Briefly, the four levels of client needs are:

1) Career Counseling

This is a career counseling model, and it assumes that most of what our clients need from us is information and skill-building related to career issues.

2) Emotionally-Focused Career Counseling

Job search, job loss and career exploration are all freighted with emotions for our clients—hope, desire, anxiety, fear, and anger all affect clients at various points of the career process. Counselors need to help clients navigate their emotional responses to the career process.

3) Therapeutic Career Counseling

Many clients bring issues that are not strictly career-related into career counseling—everything from an impending divorce to major depression to a long-standing problem with mind-numbing verbosity. When these issues threaten to derail the career process, they must be addressed.

4) Therapy with a Career Focus

Clients end up in crisis—panic attacks, manic episodes, suicidal ideation, the sudden death of a loved one. Clients need help connecting with the necessary resources without losing sight of their career goals.

ICC, the Savvy Career Counselor Series and This Guide

The Integrative Career Counseling model informs everything I do as a counselor. The Savvy Career Counselor series addresses the day-to-day challenges that career counselors and coaches encounter in their work with clients. The series is intended to be useful to all career counselors and coaches, whether or not they find the ICC model compelling, so aside from this section, you won't find ICC mentioned in *The Savvy Career Counselor: Coaching Clients on Salary and other Workplace Negotiations*.

However, if you do use ICC, or want to begin incorporating the ICC model into your work, this is an Integrative Career Counseling guide, and provides techniques and approaches for addressing Levels 1 and 2 of client needs: Career Counseling and Emotionally-Focused Career Counseling. Here's a quick key to how ICC and this guide fit together:

Level 1: Career Counseling

Because negotiating salaries and other workplace issues is a staple of almost all career counseling, you will find a wealth of material to support your work at Level 1.

Level 2: Emotionally-Focused Career Counseling

Level 2 addresses clients' emotional needs, and you will find that this guide frequently comments on how emotions affect a client's ability and or willingness to negotiate salary and other issues. Throughout the guide you will find techniques for helping clients manage and modulate their emotions. This guide will help you work with clients who have intense emotional reactions to salary negotiation process. They will be delighted to discover that their anxiety and fear are normal, and that you can help them deal with it.

Whether or not you consider yourself an Integrative Career Counselor, I hope you find this guide helpful in coaching your clients to improve their workplace negotiating skills.

Karen James Chopra

Table of Contents

Introduction	8
Overview of This Guide	11
Chapter 1: Explaining the Game: The Concept of Leverage	14
Chapter 2: The Preparation Phase	31
Chapter 3: Dodging Salary Questions During the Interview	40
Chapter 4: The Special Case of Executive Recruiters	62
Chapter 5: Getting the Offer and Preparing to Negotiate	68
Chapter 6: Conducting a Salary Negotiation	76
Chapter 7: Handling Other Workplace Negotiations	90
Conclusion	101
Acknowledgements	102

Introduction

Many career clients arrive in our offices possessing an impressive set of accomplishments and talents. They are skilled, articulate, polished and experienced. But it is the rare client who feels confident in negotiating salary, compensation, raises, performance awards and alternative work arrangements. Even the most experienced executives are often at a loss when it comes to managing the complex negotiations around their compensation.

Clients expect their coaches and counselors to help them navigate these complicated and often sensitive situations. But many of their coaches and counselors are also uncomfortable with negotiations, because, let's face it, very few of us spend a lot of time either in negotiations or coaching for negotiations.

I came to career counseling after more than a decade with the U.S. Government. I changed careers because my job wasn't a good fit for me—the role of trade policy specialist and negotiator meant that I spent a lot of time with paper, not people. But the enduring gift of my first career is that I spent a lot of time in negotiations, working with talented and gifted negotiators who served as my mentors. After I left the government and started working with career clients, I realized how valuable that negotiating experience was to me. Since I had spent so many years watching negotiations play out, looking for leverage, weighing out how hard to push for a given outcome, I had developed a framework that I used to analyze and prepare for negotiations. I discovered that the framework could be distilled into easily explained concepts and techniques that I could teach to most of my clients in a session or two.

If you work on career issues, you already coach clients on various workplace negotiations, and you probably work intuitively with many of the concepts described here. This guide will take what you do intuitively and make it fully conscious, expanding your range, and providing concepts and tools for you to pass along to your clients. You will be able to explain the negotiating process to clients, and guide them, step-by-step, through any negotiation.

Becoming a confident negotiations coach is a wonderful skill to add to your portfolio. Negotiations are often about dollars, so clients will be able to see exactly how valuable your assistance can be the their bottom line. I worked with one client who made two career moves in three years, each time to a more senior position. I coached her extensively on negotiating her compensation for both jobs. After she got her second job, she observed, "I've doubled my salary in three years, all because I asked for more money." Not every client will have that much success in improving her compensation, but most of them will be delighted at what they have accomplished, and thrilled with what you have empowered them to do.

Overview of this Guide

Clients are usually emotional when they approach any type of negotiation. If it is a salary negotiation, they are often anxious, and sometimes they are terrified—afraid to negotiate, because they may lose the position; afraid not to, because they need more money. For negotiation of an exit package, a client may be feeling angry about the impending separation. Since any type of powerful emotion will affect a client's ability to negotiate effectively, we, as their coach or counselor, have to be ready to help the client manage and modulate his or her emotions.

> **Clients need help managing their emotional responses if they are to negotiate effectively.**

One key way we help clients manage emotions is to adapt our coaching to what we know about the impact of emotion on the human brain. Since powerful emotions interfere with memory and recall, the process of teaching clients how to negotiate must be broken down into manageable pieces.

This guide is divided into chapters that cover what a client will need to know at each stage of the salary negotiation process. The final chapter will apply what you have learned to other types of workplace negotiations. If you want your clients to be able to execute all the necessary steps of an effective negotiation, make sure you break the process down into these manageable pieces. Here is a quick chapter overview:

Chapter 1: Explaining the Game: The Concept of Leverage

Until clients understand the negotiating game, which is all about developing and using leverage, they will be poor players. By training our clients to recognize and manage leverage, we prepare them to win the various rounds of the negotiating game.

Chapter 2: The Preparation Phase

Without our coaching, many clients don't even play the first round of the negotiating game, which occurs before the first interview happens. This section focuses on what clients need to do in the early stages of the job search to research and prepare.

Chapter 3: Dodging Salary Questions During the Interview

Clients know they aren't supposed to answer questions about salary, but don't know how to put that knowledge into practice. In this section, we cover all the different ways clients can dodge salary questions, as well as what to do when they can't.

Chapter 4: The Special Case of Executive Recruiters

Recruiters require special handling, because certain types of recruiters can be an exception to the rule about not disclosing salary information.

Chapter 5: Getting the Offer and Preparing to Negotiate

In the excitement of getting an offer, too many clients sabotage any chance of a serious negotiation by either accepting the offer, or launching into a negotiation without preparation. This section focuses on coaching clients on how to wait, and what to do to prepare for the final negotiation.

Chapter 6: Conducting a Salary Negotiation

The actual negotiation makes clients nervous, for good reason: this is a delicate time. They require intense and specific coaching on how to approach their employer, and this section provides that information.

Chapter 7: Handling Other Workplace Negotiations

The same concepts apply to other workplace negotiations, such as requesting a raise or a bonus, negotiating an alternate work schedule or a severance package. This section provides guidance on how to coach clients to adapt what they know about negotiations to these situations.

Chapter 1: Explaining the Game: The Concept of Leverage

"I know I'm not supposed to answer questions about salary or salary history, but when someone asks point blank, what am I supposed to do?" I hear this complaint over and over again from clients when we approach the topic of salary negotiation. The clients are correct to complain. That piece of advice is useless unless the client understands the concept of leverage and how to both use it and defend it during the various stages of the negotiating process.

Let's start with the concept of leverage. Think back to your high school physics class. A lever is a simple tool that allows you to lift or move more weight than you could with only your body strength. Negotiating leverage allows you to get more from the other party than you could without the leverage. In salary negotiations, leverage allows the client to extract the maximum compensation from the employer—often, more than the employer initially intended to offer. To be successful in negotiating salary and compensation, clients must understand leverage and how to use it.

> **Negotiating leverage allows the client to get more from the employer.**

The ultimate goal of a salary negotiation is to deploy the maximum amount of leverage to get the highest level of salary and compensation from the prospective employer, while (and herein lies the challenge) making them like it, or at least not resent it.

Until your client understands the overarching concept of leverage, what creates it, how to preserve it and how to deploy it, they will not negotiate the best possible compensation package, no matter how much good advice you give them.

Who Has Leverage?

Most clients have some leverage—enough so that they can probably ask for something during a salary negotiation. However, a few clients are in such competitive environments that they have little leverage, but I still encourage those clients to ask for something that seems doable. It's always a good experience to have an employer offer a bit extra to secure the client's acceptance of the job. A few clients, due to their expertise or timing factors, have enormous leverage, and I encourage them to use it to the maximum effect, because the next time around the situation will be different. It doesn't matter how much leverage your client has. Your goal is to assist your client in protecting and maximizing the available leverage from the moment the client launches a search.

To help you explain the concept of leverage, use the figure below, called, "The Chopra Leverage Graph for Salary Negotiations[tm]"[1]. I find it helpful to draw this line graph for clients so that they can visualize their leverage. The graph shows the amount of leverage on the vertical axis, and passage of time on the horizontal axis.

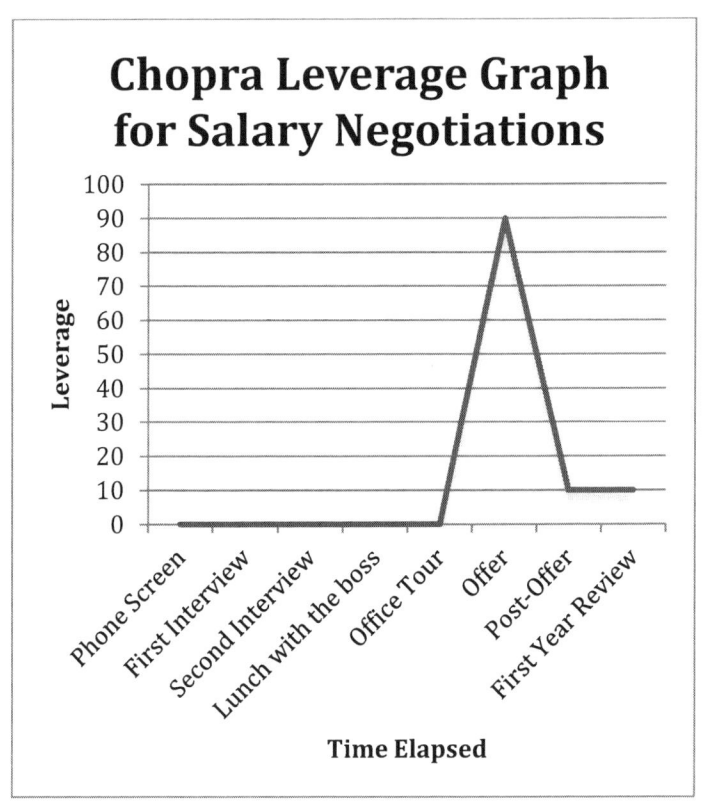

---

[1] If you use Chopra Leverage Graph with clients, please cite the source.

As you study the graph, notice a client's leverage starts at zero, and stays at zero during the screening phone call, the first interview, the second interview, the panel interview, the meet-and-greet with potential staff and the courtesy call with the CEO. In fact, the client's leverage stays at zero until the moment an offer is made, at which point, leverage spikes to its maximum level. Notice that once the offer is accepted, leverage drops back close to zero, and stays there for the remainder of the client's tenure with that company, unless other events intervene. This is the reason that it is so difficult to extract large raises or other changes to compensation after a client joins an organization—they have very little leverage.

> **The job offer is the moment of maximum leverage in any salary negotiation.**

The Leverage Graph demonstrates that the client's moment of maximum leverage is also the client's *only* moment of leverage, and it occurs once an offer has been made. All of the advice, coaching and strategies we provide to our clients should be focused on preserving leverage until an offer is made. That's why the conventional wisdom says not to talk about salary during interviews—it diminishes precious leverage for no benefit.

Once clients understand why they shouldn't be talking salary, and what they are attempting to accomplish through the various strategies we offer them, they are far more likely to attempt to dodge salary questions, and they will be better able to come up with creative answers on the fly.

The way I get my clients to visualize the leverage they are defending is to describe it as a little pile of gold dust that needs to be carefully protected throughout the interviewing process. Carelessly handing it over one or a few grains at a time is equivalent to agreeing to a salary figure tossed out during an interview. Like those weightless individual specks of dust, it will have little impact. However, bagged up together and plunked down at the right moment (when an offer is made), it can often tilt the scales in favor of more money or a more attractive offer.

I make sure that my clients and I discuss the concept of leverage, and the Chopra Leverage Graph, long before the first cover letter goes out. Events can occur quickly in a job search, and I want my clients to be forearmed and armed with knowledge. It is also helpful to discuss salary negotiation concepts, more than once, before any offers come in, because this is usually new material for a client and he or she needs time to absorb it.

Your coaching task at this stage is to develop your own mini-lecture on negotiating leverage to use with clients as early as possible. I assure you that these basic insights into the salary negotiation process will make your clients grateful that they have you in their corner.

> **Develop your own mini-lecture on leverage.**

What Creates Leverage in a Salary Negotiation?

Leverage can be created in any number of ways, many of them unique to the specific negotiation at hand. For example, if an organization must have a position filled by a certain date, then any candidate receiving an offer will have a lot of leverage in the salary negotiation. To help you and your clients think through where the leverage may lie in a given salary negotiation, here are some examples of ways leverage is created. Some of them are quite predictable; others may surprise you.

Time

Time is a key component of any negotiation. The pressure to get a deal increases as a deadline approaches. Clients often fret about how long the interview process is taking, but the silver lining is that the more time the employer invests in the candidate, the more leverage the candidate will have once an offer is made.

Look again at the graph of the leverage line. Notice that the point of maximum leverage is reached only after time has elapsed from the initial submission of an application to the offer. Time is money, which means the employer has invested significantly in this search process. The employer wants that investment to pay off with a great hire, hopefully someone who will stay for a number of years, so that the employer doesn't have to invest this kind of time again in the near

> **The time it takes to identify a job candidate generates leverage for most clients.**

future.

The passage of time represents a sunk cost to the employer—once it's spent, it's gone. By the end of a long and complicated interview process, the employer wants to have something to show for those sunk costs. Therefore, when an offer is made, the employer is invested in getting the chosen applicant to say "yes." If asked, the employer will likely grant reasonable requests for increases in the initial offer, a signing bonus, an accelerated review process, a flexible work schedule, additional vacation time, etc.

Pain and Suffering

Clients are usually so focused on their own agonizing job search that they don't focus on the suffering occurring on the other side. In many organizations, that open slot is generating a lot of extra work for existing staff, and, if the position is more senior, is endangering the organization's ability to accomplish its goals. The person responsible for filling the open slot is probably being accosted on a daily, if not hourly, basis, with the question: "When are you going to hire someone to fill that job?" The hiring manager is under pressure to get someone into the job, pressure that will only increase as the interview process moves along. All that pain and suffering translates into leverage once an offer is made—everyone wants the pain to stop, and will do whatever it takes.

> **Interviewing is hard on employers too—they want the process to be done, and this confers leverage.**

Information

Nations invest heavily in intelligence operations because information can be such a powerful tool. Your clients can be on the lookout for ways to make information work for them. One of the easiest ways to use information to create leverage is to withhold data that will increase the employer's leverage—salary data.

Economists report that given complete information, markets will do a good job of accurately pricing a commodity. But it is actually quite difficult to find good information on salary levels. This is the reason why there is so much money to be made in producing salary and compensation surveys for large corporations. These organizations are desperate for good data, which will allow them to set their salaries at appropriate levels—not too high, and not too low. Salary surveys are expensive, however, so even large corporations won't invest in salary surveys for every job (they often focus on senior management positions or specific technical skills).

Most employers, lacking the financial wherewithal to order up a salary survey whenever they hire for a new position, are flying blind. They know what they make, they know what they pay, but they aren't so sure what other people make or what other employers pay.

This uncertainty creates leverage, as long as it is maintained. The employer isn't sure what they need to pay for a quality employee, therefore they base their decision on two data points that they have access to: 1) what the previous incumbent in that position was paid, and 2) what the current candidates were paid in their previous positions.

I strongly encourage my clients *not* to provide that second data point—their previous salary. Keeping that information confidential decreases the employer's information and therefore increases the client's leverage.

> **The employer's uncertainty about what to pay for any given position generates leverage.**

When a candidate asks for a salary offer to be increased, the employer doesn't know whether the request reflects the market, or whether the candidate is just being an effective negotiator. It doesn't matter, in the end. Without knowing exactly what the market is paying for this position, the employer will often accede to a candidate's request to increase the amount of the offer.

This is why we tell our clients not to discuss salary history or requirements during the interview. We ask them to control this information so they can maximize their leverage. Once our clients understand the motivation, they learn to gracefully dodge requests for salary information, and they become much more willing and determined participants in this phase of the negotiation. When we begin coaching them on specific techniques on how to dodge salary questions, our clients become avid listeners and learners, because they understand how dodging salary questions connects to the process of getting the best deal.

Getting the Time to Shine

Managing information is not always about minimizing how much information the employer gets. The more information an employer has about how well qualified the candidate is for the position, the more likely the employer will be to improve an offer when asked.

This strategy is more than simply declining to talk about salary. We want our clients to have the opportunity to make the employer fall in love with them as a potential employee. In almost all cases, this happens as the employer gets more information about what the employee brings to the table. To maximize the flow of positive tidbits to the employer, the discussion needs to continue.

Nothing will stop that process of "getting to know you" faster than an early disclosure of a high salary figure. Much as I may love the fashions I see at Neiman Marcus, I don't often shop there, because I know my credit card will burst into flames if I actually try to purchase something. So rather than risk falling in love with an outfit that I either cannot afford or that I will regret once my spouse sees the bill, I walk on by and shop someplace where I know I can afford the price point.

> **Candidates who look too "expensive" will quickly be eliminated from the interview process.**

Employers are no different. If a candidate looks too expensive, the employer will simply stop shopping, and move on to a candidate that is more affordable. If we want our clients to be in a position to demonstrate to an employer that they are perfect for the job, and to benefit from that perfection by negotiating a great compensation package, we have to persuade them to hold on tight to salary data that may eliminate them from the interview process in the early stages.

Lack of Equivalent Candidates

Sometimes an employer finds two fabulous candidates for a job, and the struggle is to pick the best one. In situations where there is a second candidate that is viewed by the employer as identical in both skills, and more importantly, fit, then a candidate may not have much leverage—push too hard, and the employer may decide to make an offer to the other candidate.

It's more likely to be the case, however, that one candidate emerges from the interview process that is clearly superior to the others in terms of skills, ambition, personality, and fit. Having spent long hours with the various candidates, the employer has become convinced that there is really only one acceptable candidate for the job. The employer makes an offer, hoping and praying that the candidate will say, "yes," because there really isn't an acceptable fallback candidate. If the offer is rejected, the employer will have to go back through the entire process. The costs to do this are high—more time wasted, more work left undone, and the possibility exists that they still won't find a candidate as perfect, in their mind, as your client.

Therefore, when the offer is made, the candidate has tremendous leverage, because the employer will do anything in their power to get the candidate to take the job.

The "Clean Desk" Fantasy

Another important factor in leverage is the employer's fantasy about all the work that a new hire is going to take off the hiring manager's desk. A position is being filled either because someone has vacated a position, or because the workload has expanded so dramatically that more staff are required. In either case, there is more work than workers, and the hiring manager is often feeling the stress and pressure of the undone work. As a strong candidate emerges, the employer inevitably starts imagining the tasks and assignments that the candidate will take on once on board.

Imagining they see the light at the end of the tunnel, the employer now has a strong incentive to make it happen by being as flexible as possible when the chosen candidate makes requests. More leverage.

Effects on the Hiring Manager's Reputation

Hiring and retaining strong staff are the hallmark of a good manager. The inability to fill a vacant position or the failure to bring on board the desired candidate is often viewed negatively by more senior managers. If consensus has emerged inside an organization that a candidate is a good fit, the hiring manager will be under pressure to complete the hire, resulting in more leverage for the candidate once the offer is made.

The Scarce Commodity

If a candidate possesses skills or experience, or even personality traits such as enthusiasm, calm, creativity, and disposition, which are hard to find in one package, that automatically increases the candidate's leverage. If the employer cannot find what they need anywhere else, then the candidate can extract quite large concessions during salary negotiations. Hence the outrageous salaries paid to computer programmers during the tech boom of the early 2000s—there was a perceived shortage of programming skills, and so individuals who possessed programming skills could name their price.

Emotional Intelligence

Nice guys do NOT finish last when it comes to salary negotiations. If a candidate is viewed as having both the skills necessary for the task, and is viewed as being emotionally intelligent—that is, adept at managing relationships and emotions on the job, then the employer will often work very hard to get an affirmative response to a job offer. Employers will sometimes select a candidate who is slightly less qualified on paper but clearly superior in terms of emotional intelligence because they understand that a team's functioning often depends as much on the interpersonal skills of various staff members as on their "hard" skills.

In fact, employers have been known to hire the candidate they like more, rather than the candidate who is more skilled. Being perceived as someone who gets along well with a range of people often gives the client additional leverage. When the employer looks forward to working with that candidate, they will be amenable to requests to modify a job offer in favor of that candidate.

One concrete way for our clients to demonstrate their emotional intelligence—their ability to handle difficult issues with aplomb—is for them to be savvy salary negotiators. Even if an employer is chagrined at not getting the salary data they would like, they are often impressed by how calmly and gracefully the client is handling the pressure. (Many of those hiring managers may be wondering why they couldn't do such a good job when they interviewed for their current position!)

Other Factors Contributing to Leverage

Each client brings their own unique profile to the negotiation—but the factors above are usually present in most salary situations. The important thing is to evaluate the factors that will increase or diminish a client's leverage, and develop strategies and tactics to maximize leverage in any given situation.

For example, I once had a client who had a specific knowledge base about a fairly esoteric regulation. An employer that was hoping to win a large, long-term federal contract that dealt with this esoteric regulation was courting him. The request for proposal (RFP) required that firms bidding on this federal contract have someone on staff with this specific expertise. The close date on the bid was approaching. The company had no alternative to my client. My client asked for, and received, an offer that he later learned placed him among the top-earners in the company. Of course, it helped that the employer revealed all of this information prior to the offer—the information increased my client's leverage exponentially.

It isn't possible to know exactly how much leverage an individual client has. The goal is to consciously look for things that may increase leverage, and manage these factors during a salary negotiation.

Preserving Leverage

Once your clients understand what leverage is, and how it is created, you can help them focus on ways to protect their own little pile of gold dust until the optimum moment arrives to place the whole pile on the scales. Understanding what they are trying to accomplish in avoiding any discussion of salary during the interview process makes clients highly coachable on specific techniques. They know exactly what mastery of that technique will mean in terms of leverage. It also empowers the client to adapt and be nimble as the interview process moves forward. Most negotiations—such as buying a car or a house, or signing a trade agreement—allow us to have a team and to call upon expert advice. Salary negotiations are unique in requiring the candidate to negotiate alone. We can coach them, but we can't do it for them.

Clients need the most intensive coaching around the topic of preserving leverage until the offer is made, because there are so many ways that leverage can be diminished.

> **Clients need intensive coaching on specific ways to preserve and manage leverage through the interview process.**

    I break down the task of preserving leverage into four steps: pre-interview, interview, offer and negotiating the offer. This makes it more manageable for the client, because he or she only has to focus on the tactics required for one phase at a time. The next chapter focuses on how to coach clients to prepare for salary negotiations.

Chapter 2: The Preparation Phase

Once the client understands the concept of negotiating leverage, I begin coaching them through the first round of the game, which is the period before the client has any interviews. At this stage of the process, I have two main coaching goals:

1) Gathering salary information.
2) Protecting salary information during the networking phase

The most successful salary negotiations are the result of a process that begins when the job search begins. Most clients are unaware of the opportunities and pitfalls they face at this early stage, so helping them think through various possibilities and prepare appropriate responses is an important task for the coach and counselor. For many clients, it is a life-changing experience to learn the rules of the salary negotiation game and discover that they can be competent players.

> **The most successful salary negotiations start the moment the job search begins.**

Gathering Information

As we begin to map out the client's job search. I make it a point to write out networking scripts that the client can use. In those scripts, I make sure to include questions about salary ranges. While the client is reading through job postings, I encourage them to capture and record any scraps of salary information that are out there. Any information that can be assembled about the probable salary range for a position will set the client up to be successful during the negotiation phase.

> **Clients need to ask everyone they talk to about salary ranges.**

As I mentioned earlier, it's hard to get good salary information, but if you coach your clients to ask the right questions during their networking calls and meetings, they will enter the salary negotiation phase with more information at their disposal than the average employer, which will increase their leverage.

Encourage your clients to ask everyone they network with questions like "What's the salary range for this position?" or, "What salary range should I be looking at, based on my qualifications or experience?"

Make sure you coach the clients beyond those questions, too, because most people will decline to answer the first time: "Oh, I don't know." Most people know more than they think they do about likely salary ranges, so urge your clients to follow up with a prompt such as: "Just give me a ballpark figure."

When prompted to give a "ballpark estimate," most people will draw on what they know about their own salary, the salaries of people they supervise, the industry as a whole, and give a range: "Somewhere between $60,000 and $90,000." That is all your client needs. By itself, that salary range is a highly questionable number, but if your clients keep asking each person they contact the same set of questions, they will soon compile enough data to have confidence in the salary range for the specific position being sought out.

Here is where preparing for salary negotiations from the outset can really pay off for your client. It may be weeks or months before an offer comes in, but whenever it does, your clients will be ready to leverage the research done in the early phase of the search. Clients don't necessarily understand this at first, so I always give them an example (see below) to help them connect their current questions on salary ranges with the eventual salary negotiation.

> **Give clients examples of how they will use salary research in the negotiation process.**

I usually tell clients a story about how that salary data will be used. For example, I'll say, "Let's look at how a client we'll call "Mindy" uses her research on salary ranges. When presented with an offer that seems low, Mindy can say, "Based on my research, the salary range for this position is $60,000 to $90,000. Given the amount of experience I have in the field, I was expecting to come in close to the top of that range."

Notice what Mindy is doing. She is using information gathered during the pre-interview phase to increase her leverage over the employer. This is not an imaginary number. Mindy has reasonable confidence that her statement is based in fact, therefore, she can make the assertion calmly and non-defensively. The employer may not be able to meet Mindy's request, but they may offer something else of value to make up for the fact that they are falling short on salary.

> **Research into salary ranges at the beginning of the job search leads to increased leverage in a salary negotiation.**

This negotiating stance—"based on my research, I was expecting X"—is only possible if the client begins gathering information from the outset of the job search. Most clients don't think that far in advance, and so one of our contributions is laying the early groundwork for successful salary negotiations.

Protecting Salary Information in The Pre-Interview Phase

Most clients know that they shouldn't tell employers in an interview what their salary expectations are, but those same clients will often happily disclose their salary demands or salary history to people they consider friends during their networking. This is often done defensively—"I won't take anything under $175,000" or, "I won't take another job that pays only $45,000." As understandable as these statements are, I encourage clients not to talk about their salary history or requirements even during the networking process.

> **Clients need to keep salary information confidential from everyone.**

There are two main reasons for being coy about salary data. The first is that information travels, and juicy information, like how much Susan was making at her last job, travels faster. Many of our clients are job searching in relatively small professional worlds. We encourage them to network because you never know who knows whom. I encourage clients to keep mum on money for the exact same reason. If Susan has let her network know that she made $175,000 in her last job, and her interviewer has learned that through the network, the interviewer may be disinclined to offer the full $225,000 budgeted for this position—even $200,000 will be a nice bump for Susan. Susan wants to preserve her leverage, so she needs to be careful that her networking isn't working against her.

The second reason for withholding salary information is that it should not be up to the network to decide which jobs clients hear about. If David has been very clear about the size of his price tag, then a networking contact may decide not to pass on the perfect job opening because the current salary associated with it is $10,000 below David's stated minimum.

It can be painful to be forwarded job postings that are not at the appropriate level. Many of my clients feel insulted and diminished when a contact passes along a lower level posting, and so they announce their salary level in an attempt to emphasize their seniority. I encourage them to revisit their elevator speech and ensure it conveys their qualifications accurately, rather than go for the quick but unhelpful fix of attaching a specific price to their expertise.

Besides, it's never bad to be notified that a company has an opening. Even if it's not at the right level, the client can contact the hiring manager and start a conversation. Just the fact that someone in your network thinks of you when they see a job opening is a good sign.

Coach your clients on how to avoid disclosing salary information even during their networking conversations. I find it helpful to work with clients to develop basic talking points that they can use or modify as needed. In the case of networking contacts, if the client doesn't raise the issue of salary, the networking contact probably won't either. However, if a client is asked about salary requirements, they should say something like: "It's too early to be deciding on a number—I'm still doing my research, and I think I'll be flexible for the right position, but that reminds me, I wanted to get your sense of what the salary range would be for this type of position."

If anyone, at any point in the process, has the temerity to ask point blank, "What do you make now?" I encourage clients to react as if someone has asked an impertinent question (because they have!): "That's personal!"

Here is an example of Sonja effectively handling a too-personal question about her current salary from someone she doesn't know well. Remember, Sonja doesn't want to shut down the entire conversation, just the question about what she makes. She certainly doesn't want to offend her new networking contact. This is how she rebuffs the specific question, while moving the conversation in a more helpful direction: "Well, that's personal information and I don't share that, but I did want to get your sense of the salary range for this position." Sonja has managed this so skillfully that the conversation is likely to flow on with barely a hiccup.

Maintaining Leverage in Online Applications

Online applications are a major obstacle to preserving leverage in the pre-interview stage, but since they cannot be avoided entirely, we have to help our clients think through the implications of the salary number they choose to give. Very often, just the process of weighing the pros and cons of each choice will help the client feel more comfortable with the number that they finally plug into the online application.

I hate online applications. Almost all of them have a place for salary requirements, and those boxes are formatted so that the client must enter a number. They are a "required" field, so the client cannot leave it blank.

> **Online applications can diminish negotiating leverage—handle with care.**

The best way around this problem is for our clients to find jobs via effective networking, rather than by focusing their search on online postings. If clients are constantly running into the problem of having to list their salary in online applications, they are probably spending too much time responding to want ads and not enough time networking

But sometimes even good networking leads to the dreaded online application. I usually encourage clients to list a salary that they can live with, but that isn't either the top or the absolute bottom of their scale. This is where the pre-interview research can pay off—if the client has got enough salary data, he or she may be able to estimate the best number to include. For online applications, the greater risk is being automatically eliminated from further consideration for being "too expensive." It's less likely that a low salary figure will get an application tossed out, hence the advice to use a number in the middle of the client's range.

If a client has already interviewed, and has been sent back to fill out the online application, then the risk of looking too expensive is diminished: the company has already determined that they want to speak with the client. In cases where the online application is used to follow up on first interviews, I encourage clients to push the number closer to the top of their range. Often, the online application is the way the company keeps records, and it's possible that the salary information won't be looked at too closely.

> **Clients are not bound by salary requirements listed in online application.**

Finally, clients are not bound by what they list in an online application. After completing the interview process, it is quite possible that a candidate will want more money to move to the new position. It is perfectly legitimate to ask for more money than was listed in the online application. The employer may balk, but the client can justifiably say that she has more information now, and is better able to assess what her salary requirements are vis-à-vis this position.

Chapter Three: Dodging Salary Questions During the Interview

Make sure your client is ready when called for an interview. Does your client understand the concept of leverage and done everything possible up to this point to maximize leverage? Is the concept of the precious pile of gold dust understood and that it could be at high risk during the interview process if not handled properly? Has your client been coached on the tactics and techniques that will help get him or her through this critical stage? Let's look at what you need to teach your client to do during the interview process.

Don't talk about salary.

It's not enough to remind a client not to talk about salary; you have to help the client think through all the ways the issue of salary could come up. I can't tell you how many clients have told me that they raised the issue of salary in the interview by asking what a position pays. So remind your clients that a question like that is not going to help them. Even if the interviewer is caught unawares and actually answers the question, the very next question coming back across the table will be either "What salary are you looking for?" or "Is that acceptable to you?" Both questions are ones the client wants to avoid.

It is vital that you explicitly tell clients not to ask about salary. Many people are under the mistaken impression that they must ask about salary during the interview process, because that is a critical piece of information about the job. It feels strange to most people to have no idea what a position will pay, even as they go through interview after interview. But your clients will understand the concept of leverage and the implications of the leverage graph, so will be better prepared to tolerate not knowing about salary for a little while longer. The client will, of course, need to know how much the position pays before accepting it, but if the information is not forthcoming in the interview the best advise is to keep mum and sit tight.

> **Clients should never ask about the salary during interviews.**

Don't accept a salary offered during the interview

Interviewers will often offer up the salary during the course of the interview, and this is another trap that you have to help your clients sidestep. You don't want a client to accidentally agree to the figure out of surprise. If the number isn't significantly off base, the temptation to say, "OK" in response to the interviewer's statement can be intense. Indeed, if the number is high enough, clients may be tempted to respond with enthusiasm: "That's great!" The only problem is that essentially concludes the salary negotiation. The client has told the employer that the stated amount is acceptable. Imagine the little pile of gold dust blowing away in a hurricane force gale wind. Gone.

> **Warn clients not to accept salaries offered during the interview.**

If the salary stated is disappointing, then the temptation is to argue or give up in disgust. There is no point in attempting to move the number at this stage—the client has zero leverage. It is quite possible that the client won't take the position at this salary, but that doesn't mean there isn't value in continuing the interview process. The company may voluntarily increase the amount after seeing how fabulous your client is. Or there may be a more senior position that will open up, and the client will be called back to interview for that.

> **When told what a position pays, the right answer is simply: "That's good to know."**

The right thing to say when a salary number hits the table is, "That's good to know, thank you." And then the client should immediately ask a question that moves the conversation on to another topic: "Might I ask about the upcoming annual conference, and what you expect from this position in regards to the conference?" If your clients just learn the phrase "That's good to know," they will be able to dodge this pitfall successfully.

Be Ready to Dodge Questions About Salary

Dodging questions about salary is a real art, and you want your client to be good at it. During the interview is a bad time to practice dodging techniques, so get your client to rehearse ahead of time.

> **Dodging salary questions during an interview is a three-step process.**

Learning to dodge salary questions during an interview requires mastering a three-step process. Clients will absorb this process better if they learn it with you and then practice it again and again on their own. Because it takes time to get comfortable with dodging salary questions, I usually make this a part of my interview preparation process, which I begin as soon as the client starts applying for jobs. If possible, you want to avoid cramming these techniques into a client's brain the day before the interview.

We have to coach our clients with detailed and specific instructions. Even with clients as leverage-savvy as ours, it does not help them to simply instruct them not to answer salary questions. What are they supposed to do? Put their hands over their ears, close their eyes, hum, and say in a sing-song voice, "I can't hear you"? Your client is going to have to say *something*. If it is not the best answer to the question, it had better be something good.

In response to any questions about salary, the client needs to execute a three-step process:

1) Decline to answer the specific question on salary.
2) Answer the more general question.
3) Ask a question.

That's a lot to accomplish in the pressure cooker of an interview. Let's imagine coaching "Zach" through this three-step dance.

> **Step One: Decline to answer specific questions on salary.**

In the first step, Zach needs to quickly decline to answer any questions about salary, because sharing salary information will diminish his leverage. Zach chooses to go with: "That's personal information and I don't give that out." (I'll go over other possible dodges below). Zach has to do more than just refuse to answer the salary question—he has to keep the interviewer from asking again. Zach can't keep the interviewer from coming back to the salary question eventually, but he can make the interviewer work harder to get back to the salary question, and he accomplishes this by holding the floor and responding to the question behind the interviewer's question, which is: "Can we afford you?"

> **Step Two: Answer the implied question: "Can we afford you?"**

Below you will find a range of possible answers to the implied affordability question. Zach elects to say: "I'm sure salary won't be an issue if everything else falls into place," completing step two of the "salary dodge dance." However, Zach still isn't out of the woods. For step three, he needs to toss out an open-ended question that sends the conversation as far away from the salary topic as possible. The hope is that the conversation will move on, and salary won't come up again.

> **Step 3: Ask an open-ended question about a completely unrelated topic.**

As you can see, the "salary dodge dance" is complicated. Our clients will be unable to execute all these steps in quick succession unless they are coached about what to do and how to do it, and then practice. I go over these points with clients, and then suggest that they prepare a series of flashcards that contain various formulations of the salary question. Either alone or with a partner, the client can pull a question from the pile, and then answer it out loud. Verbalizing the response is critical, because the client is working on both the language and the speed and fluidity of delivery. There can be no breaths or pauses until the client has executed all three steps:

1.) Dodge
2.) Respond to the implied question
3.) Ask a question about a new topic.

I tell clients I don't care how inelegantly they do the dance; I just want them to keep talking until they have fired off that final question.

Notice that this is a lot of work for you and your client. Clients are much more likely to do the all of the preparatory work if they fully understand why it is necessary. That is why it is necessary for us to start negotiation coaching long before a client's first interview is scheduled.

Ways to Decline to Answer the Salary Question

We can't be with our clients as they dodge salary questions, and it is impossible to know precisely how the issue will come up, so rather than telling clients exactly what to say, I give clients a mix and match menu of dodges, alternate answers and good questions. When the dreaded salary question comes up, here are some ways to decline to answer it.

"It's too early to talk salary."
Particularly in the early stages of the interview process, this is a good answer because it is too early. The client doesn't know much about the job and it's requirements, and so

determining what salary would be sufficient inducement to take the job is difficult.

"That's personal information."

If interviewers ask direct questions about current salary or salary history, I encourage clients to say something such as: "I don't give out that information," or, "That's personal information." I particularly like this response because it is one that can be repeated multiple times. If it is information that isn't shared the first time the question is asked, it stays that way. It has the additional benefit of being true. Really, would you tell someone you've just met exactly what you make?

"I'm flexible."

When an interviewer inquires about a client's salary requirements, "I'm flexible" or "They are flexible" is a good, non-committal response. Remember, the goal here is to avoid providing a number without shutting down the conversation, and this response is vague enough to accomplish both of those goals.

Ways to Answer the Implied Question: "Can we afford you?"

It is not enough to dodge the question, however. It would be easy for an interviewer to brush any of the statements above aside and ask the salary question more forcefully. To keep the conversation moving, and to avoid looking difficult, the client must answer the interviewer's question. Those are the rules of the job interview—the interviewer asks, the interviewee responds.

I coach clients to answer the question that is implied in the salary question; what I call, "the question behind the question." The interviewer is really trying to figure out whether the candidate's salary expectations fall into the salary range that the company is prepared to pay. If the answer is no, the company wants to stop wasting time looking at a candidate who is too expensive.

> **Clients can choose the salary question they would prefer to answer.**

Here are a few ways that the client can answer the implied question:

"It will all work out......"

Sometimes, it works to simply assert that salary won't be a problem: "I'm sure if everything else falls into place, salary won't be an issue."

"Based on my research, I'm confident it won't be an issue."

In many cases, your client will have done enough research to be confident that the company will pay an adequate salary. Referring to that research is another way to respond to the employer's concerns that salary will be a problem: "Based on my research, Widget Inc. pays its employees market rate salaries, and you have already told me about your great benefits package. If I'm fortunate to be selected for this position, I don't imagine salary is going to be an issue."

"I need more information."

It is always legitimate for the client to observe that there has not been enough information provided at this point in the conversation. This is best delivered with a focus on meeting expectations: "I don't have enough information on what you are hoping I will be able to do for you in this position."

Questions to Change the Subject

So far, so good, but your client still isn't in the clear. It is all too easy for the interviewer to brush aside these neutral statements and re-ask the salary question. In order for this dance to work, the client must execute the final step, which is to ask a question that will change the subject.

The question that the client asks can be on any topic. The only rule is that it cannot be a yes/no question. That won't change the topic. The question should begin with one of the following words: what, where, who, when or how. (Questions that begin with "why" are always a bit tricky, since they can sound aggressive or challenging.)

In preparing clients for this part of the salary dodge dance, I help them develop an extensive list of questions for the employer. I encourage them to type up the list and keep it in their binder so that they can refer to it during the interview. That way, instead of struggling to recall a meaty question to toss out to the interviewer, the client simply needs to look at the list of prepared questions and pick one.

Here are a few suggested questions, plus an explanation for how to reprogram questions that are often asked in an interview so that they can be asked of an interviewer.

"If I take this job, and have an outstanding first year, what will I have accomplished?"
This is one of my favorite interview questions. It makes the interviewer think, and it provides the client with insight into how well thought out the job requirements are, and it usually provokes a good discussion that keeps the salary question at bay.

"How is performance evaluated in this organization?"
A nice segue from salary issues—let's focus on what you think constitutes a high performer.

"What is the agenda for this position for the first 90 days? What has to be accomplished right out of the gate?"
Demonstrates a strong interest in understanding the boss' priorities.

"Who would be my most important counterparts and stakeholders, both within and outside of the organization?"
Most jobs have a wide range of stakeholders, so this is an excellent question to move the discussion far beyond salary.

Turning-the-Table Questions
I encourage clients to reformulate questions that employers typically ask. This often produces thought-inducing questions that do a very effective job of changing the subject. "Where do you see this organization heading in five years?" "What would you say is the greatest strength of this organization?" "What has been your greatest success in the past several years?" "Where do you think this organization has stumbled recently, and what are you doing to address that?"

> **Clients should feel free to ask employers the same tough questions they have to answer.**

Employers ask these questions because they are hard, and the answers are often revealing. For those same reasons, these questions are good ones to ask an interviewer.

Putting it Together

Here are several examples of what the three steps look like when executed together. I usually model these types of statements for my clients so that they can see how to put all the pieces together. It also helps them to understand the level of fluency they are striving for in their individual practice sessions.

"Sally" is in the middle of her initial phone screen, and the interviewer asks: "What are your salary requirements?"

Sally responds: "It's a little early to talk about salary requirements. I need to know more about the position, and what you hope I will be able to accomplish for you. Can you tell me a little bit about why the position is open and the major challenges and issues you expect the selected candidate to address?"

"Derek" is in his third interview, and as his interviewer is showing him around the office, he casually asks Derek: "So, what's your current salary?"

Derek doesn't miss a beat as he says: "I don't give out that information, but if you are asking because you are concerned that salary may become an issue, let me assure you that, if everything else falls into place, I don't expect that to happen. You have a terrific office here. Tell me, what are your goals for this department going forward—in the next year, two years, and five years?"

"Mitchell" is talking with the Human Resources Director and she asks what he makes now. Mitchell nods and smiles, "That's personal information, and I don't give that out, but if you are concerned about salary becoming an issue, let me assure you that I have done my research and am confident it won't be. I notice that this job has been posted for several months now. What are you looking for in your candidate that has been hard to find? "

Notice how nicely it all works together. The candidate is declining to answer the salary question directly, but does address the implied question with a positive and upbeat response before immediately moving the conversation onto a new topic. If the candidate is lucky, this is the only time salary will be addressed.

Let me reiterate: It is critical that the client not relinquish the floor until the topic-changing question has been launched. Not everyone will be as smooth as Sally or Derek or Mitchell, and it doesn't matter. The most important thing is that the client follows Sally's example and not pause, even to take a breath, until she has asked the question. She can hesitate, and stumble, and "ummmm" all she wants, but she cannot stop the flow of sound throughout the entire dodge.

Deirdre is a nervous interviewer, so when the salary question comes her heart starts pounding. "Um, gee, that's personal information, I, uh, don't give that, um, out, but I think you probably wonder....you probably want to know if I am expecting too much money for this, um, position. I can tell you that I can't see... I don't expect that salary is going to be an issue here. I wonder...can you, um, can we talk about....What I mean to say is, can we talk about how your organization relates to Very Important Inc.? I've done lots of work with Very Important Inc. and I think my contacts can be helpful there. How much work do you do with them?"

It wasn't pretty, because Deirdre was so nervous, but she got through all three steps. She hung onto the floor until she got to her question, where she picked up steam and did a nice job of both asking a question and highlighting the relationships she brings to the table. Focus on getting your clients to execute the three steps, and don't worry about how smooth they are in expressing them.

Practice is vital to getting through the interview process without giving up important negotiating leverage. Clients can practice with you, they can practice in the shower, they can get a friend to quiz them, or use flash cards as I suggested above, but they must practice going through these three steps out loud before they get to the interview. Executing these steps is the only defense their little pile of gold dust has during the interview process.

> **Practice makes perfect. Encourage clients to practice saying various responses to salary questions out loud to improve their fluency.**

When the Dodge Doesn't Do It

Some interviewers will not take "no" for an answer when it comes to salary. Many HR professionals are required to get salary information before referring candidates for the next round of interviews. They have a list of questions in front of them, and they will keep coming back to the question until they get an answer.

In the case of executive recruiters, it is part of their mandate from the employer to provide a slate of candidates that will accept the salary the employer has settled on for the position, so they must provide detailed and accurate salary data. We'll talk about executive recruiters in a separate section, for now, let's focus on what your clients can do when dodging a salary question doesn't work.

Give your clients multiple ideas for dealing with a persistent questioner, because it's hard to know in advance what the client will encounter in the interview.

> **Prepare clients to handle persistent questions about salary.**

Push Back—Gently

I encourage clients not to be a pushover on salary information, but they have to walk a fine line, because they cannot be difficult in an interview, either. If a client has indicated that salary is a personal issue, or that it's too early to talk salary, has done so a couple of times, and the issue of salary is being raised again, then it's time to employ a new tactic.

In certain circumstances, a gentle pushback may be useful. For example, Rolando has had two interviews with a company, and has always indicated that what he makes is a personal issue. It has worked a couple of times, but now salary is coming up again. Rolando might say: "You know, you have asked me what I make several times, and I wonder if you are concerned that you are not paying market rates for this position?" Tone is everything here; this must be delivered in a non-defensive, curious way.

Delivered in the right way, this question puts the interviewer in a bit of a tight spot. First, it's a surprise, because Rolando hasn't pushed back before. Second, there isn't a good answer to this question.

Most interviewers will be surprised into reflexively denying that they are paying below market rates. If that's the case, Rolando will simply respond: "That's what I thought. Based on my research, your organization pays competitively and offers great benefits. I don't think you need to have any concerns on the salary issue. I am curious, though, about your top priorities for the first three months of this position. Ninety days in, what do you want to have been accomplished?"

Rolando has essentially closed the salary issue. The interviewer will have a hard time raising this again.

Some interviewers will double-down and insist that they need this information. In this case, Rolando can ask why—but carefully. "Really? I do want to give you all the information you need to decide I'm your candidate, but could you tell me how knowing what I make right now will help you to determine if I am the right fit for the job?"

Once again, there isn't a great answer to this question. The most likely answer is that the interviewer wants to know how pricey Rolando is as a candidate. The interviewer is unlikely to say that, but may try: "We just want to make sure that you are really interested in this position."

Rolando can give a very heartfelt response to the question: "I am very interested in this position, and the more time I spend with this organization, the more excited I am about the challenges. I have trouble imagining that salary is going to be a problem here. As I have said, I don't give out personal financial data, but what type of information would be helpful to you?"

Rolando has once again politely declined to provide salary data, but has offered the possibility of providing other data that could help the employer evaluate his candidacy.

The type of gentle pushbacks I have just described will not work in every situation. It is best with an interviewer who seems to be asking the question because it's "on the list." Many interviewers are uncomfortable asking about salary, because they hate this type of question, too.

Don't Give a Number, Give a Range

Many of our clients encounter people who, for one reason or another, must get a salary figure. If the candidate won't play ball, the candidate won't get passed on for the next round of interviews.

No one has the right to our salary information, but sometimes it is not possible to continue to refuse to provide salary data. In cases where a number must be handed over, I like the formulation proposed by John Lucht, author of *Rites of Passage at $100,00 To $1 Million+*. He suggests providing a range for recent compensation. He emphasizes that it is compensation, not salary, and that it be a range, not a number. The goal is to offer a range that brackets the probable salary for this position.

> **If the client must provide salary information, give a range, not a number.**

Faced with an interviewer who insists on having a number, Rolando might respond "Perhaps it will help if I tell you that, in recent years, my compensation has ranged from $85,000 to $175,000."

Lucht suggests that the lower number represent what the client made a few years back, and that the higher number represent the most generous description of all compensation received over the same period. He argues that such a wide range will encourage an employer to think that the candidate is in the right ballpark.

It isn't ideal, but it's still better than providing a single number. Your clients will not be able to come up with this range on the fly, so your job as a coach is to help them recognize and prepare for situations where there is no possibility of refusing to provide some form of salary data.

> **Help clients decide the salary range they will provide if it isn't possible to dodge salary questions.**

A final note here: Some companies insist that candidates provide their most recent W-2 or tax return. Companies have no legal right to this information, nor do they have a legal obligation to hire someone who doesn't comply with their requests. You will have to help clients faced with this situation figure out where they stand, and what consequences they are willing to accept for that stance. Where companies are using their power as the holder of a job opening to extract maximum data from all applicants, I remind the client that the interview process is often as good as it gets in terms of treatment, and this type of data request should be a red flag about the company.

If, however, the W-2 or tax return is requested only post-offer, as part of the final paperwork, it may be that it's simply an overzealous bureaucracy at work. If the request is made after the salary negotiation is complete, the data poses less of a threat to the job seeker. Providing a W-2 becomes a problem, of course, if the job seeker lied about salary, in which case it could be cause for termination. Hence my advice to clients is to dodge salary questions, but never lie in response to them. The consequences for any untruth told in the course of the interview process are simply too severe.

> **Don't let clients lie about salary history—the consequences are too high.**

The Executive Recruiter

When dealing with some types of executive recruiters, dodging salary questions may not be the appropriate tactic at all. Executive recruiters are such a complicated and special case that I'll address them in the next chapter.

Chapter 4: The Special Case of the Executive Recruiter

Executive recruiters are a special case. In some cases, an executive recruiter will be the one exception to our advice to clients to never talk about salary.

First, a quick reminder that there are three types of recruiters: retained, contingency, and in-house. Clients need to know which type of recruiter they are dealing with before deciding whether to disclose salary information. I am going to give a quick overview of the executive recruiter landscape here. The best in-depth discussion of handling recruiters that I have seen is in John Lucht's book *Rites of Passage at $100,00 To $1 Million+*.

> **Educate clients about types of recruiters and how to handle salary questions.**

Retained recruiters

Retained recruiters are hired by a firm or organization to conduct a search for a candidate. They have signed a contract with the client specifying the terms of the search. Traditionally, a retained recruiter gets paid if the position is filled, regardless of whether the recruiter was responsible for presenting the successful candidate. This arrangement usually means that the hiring company turns responsibility for the entire interview process over to the recruiter. If you are going to pay the recruiter no matter what, it makes sense to get the recruiter to do the vast majority of the work. Retained recruiters are traditionally paid 30-35% of the hired candidate's first year salary. The current recession has forced some changes in the executive recruiting business, especially squeezing the margins, but the overall model still works. Among the best-known retained recruiting firms are Korn/Ferry, Heidrick & Struggles, and Russell Reynolds Associates, but there are many smaller, highly reputable executive recruiting firms out there.

A retained recruiter will insist on having a client's salary requirements up front, and if the client has any interest in working with the recruiter, the client will comply. The firm has turned over the hiring process to the recruiter, and she has become the gatekeeper. One of the advantages to the firm of ceding this monopoly on hiring to the recruiter is that it gets a slate of candidates that is pre-vetted on salary (and other factors as well, such as willingness to relocate). No recruiter is going to present a candidate that will turn down the position because of salary.

The recruiter gets paid based on the candidate's first year salary, so the recruiter has a strong incentive to see that the candidate gets the highest salary that the hiring company is prepared to offer.

Since we spend so much time encouraging our clients to protect salary data, we need to coach them explicitly to handle retained recruiters differently. Although recruiters may want salary history, the most important question will be the client's salary requirements. The client should present a salary range, to maximize the chance that actual salary is bracketed within that range, and to indicate some flexibility on salary. Clients should be truthful with retained recruiters. If it's going to take a $50,000 bump to get the client to switch jobs, the client should say that up front. Once a number has been handed to the recruiter, it will be difficult to change.

> **When working with a retained recruiter, clients must provide salary requirements.**

Contingency Recruiters

Contingency recruiters often have no contractual arrangement with the firm that is hiring, or the contract is limited to payment only if the contingency recruiter's candidate is hired. If a contingency recruiter finds a candidate that fits an existing opening, the recruiter will present that candidate to the firm. If that candidate is hired, the contingency recruiter will be paid a fee.

Because the firm only pays the contingency recruiter if that recruiter's candidate is hired, there is a risk to the client in working with a contingency recruiter. If the firm has several good candidates that applied directly for the position, those candidates will be cheaper, because there is no recruiter's fee associated with the selection of those candidates. Clients should be encouraged to weigh carefully whether working with the contingency recruiter makes sense.

> **Contingency recruiters can make a client more expensive than other applicants for the same job.**

Sometimes it will make sense to work with a contingency recruiter. If the recruiter has a lead on a good position that a client has not been able to uncover through personal networking, then the client should permit the recruiter to present them to the employer. Although the client may be a more expensive candidate, at least there is a chance of being considered for the job.

Once the client has decided to work with a contingency recruiter, the rules about disclosing salary information are the same as for retained recruiters—the recruiter has every incentive to get the client the best deal, so there is little risk in providing the desired salary range.

Clients need to be coached to work with contingency recruiters. Clients are entitled to know whenever a recruiter is going to pass their resume along to a company, and are entitled to decline to have their materials presented if they aren't comfortable being represented by the recruiter for a specific position. Too often, clients are in awe of recruiters and fail to ask important questions to protect themselves.

In-House Recruiters

Many companies now use in-house recruiters to fill positions. Most are honest and straightforward. But sometimes those recruiters attempt to look like outside, retained recruiters so that unwary candidates will share salary information with them.

In-house recruiters should be treated the same as HR managers with respect to salary information. They work for the hiring company and have no incentive to see that the candidate gets top dollar. Clients should share as little salary information as possible with these recruiters.

> **Treat in-house recruiters like any other HR professional, and don't provide salary data.**

Tricks for Identifying Types of Recruiters

Telling the difference between retained, contingency and in-house recruiters can be challenging. Even big-name, retained firms will sometimes operate on a contingency basis, so the simple fact that the recruiter is with an executive search firm does not guarantee that he or she is a retained recruiter. Coach your client to ask questions to determine the type of recruiter they are dealing with. All recruiters should be asked on what basis they are working with the hiring firm. If the recruiter has been retained, in most cases, they are happy to announce that fact: "We have been retained to fill this position."

Clients should probe for more information if the recruiter uses euphemisms. "We have an arrangement," may simply mean that the recruiter has worked with this firm before on a contingency basis. "I have been asked to fill this position," might just mean the recruiter knows the HR Director, who passed along the information about the vacancy.

In the case of an in-house recruiter who is being coy about her real employer, the client may try a range of questions: "Are you in-house or retained?" "What firm do you work for?" "How many corporate clients are you currently working with?" "Who is your employer?"

Clients should be wary whenever a recruiter uses deliberately vague phrasing to describe their role. Retained recruiters are almost always delighted to announce their status, so if a recruiter is dancing around, but declining to say, "retained," then that is a clear sign that the client is dealing with either a contingency or an in-house recruiter, and the client should proceed accordingly.

Chapter Five: Getting the Job Offer and Preparing to Negotiate

Eventually, the client will make it through all of the interviews and get the phone call he or she has been waiting for: the offer of a job.

All that carefully protected leverage can vanish in an instant if the client has not been coached on how to handle an offer. For many clients, the temptation to grab the offer the instant it hits the table is overwhelming, and who can blame them? They have been searching for weeks or months, dealing with anxiety and depression, fearing that they will never work again. Of course the first instinct is to blurt: "Oh, thank God, of course I'll take it! When do I start?"

> **All that carefully protected leverage can vanish in an instant if the client has not been coached on how to handle a job offer.**

But our clients know better. They have the Leverage Graph imprinted on the back of their eyelids, and they know that their moment has arrived. So our clients will react to the offer positively and enthusiastically. They will say everything that they would like to say, except, "Yes, I'll take it."

Let's walk through "Talia's" negotiation process as an example. When Talia gets the call that she is being offered an attractive position as a research analyst with a starting salary of $42,500, she allows all her excitement to come through in her response: "That is wonderful! I am so very excited. Would you mind emailing me the offer, and send along your benefits package so that I can review it? When do you need to hear back from me?"

Talia is signaling her interest in the job, but also the fact that she isn't saying, "yes," just yet. A smart employer will recognize that it can expect a salary negotiation. And if the employer isn't smart, they will find out soon enough what Talia has in mind.

The reason for getting the offer in writing is that clients often forget the details, including the salary, the title and the start date, as soon as they hang up the phone. One client called me after getting an offer and couldn't remember whether her bonus potential was $1,500 or $15,000. The adrenaline generated by the excitement of an offer interferes with memory. So a written offer is important. It doesn't need to be a formal offer letter—a quick email with the terms of the offer is sufficient.

Clients also need to review the benefits package, because there can be some expensive surprises hidden in the differences between benefits packages. One client discovered that the new firm did not offer family health coverage, reducing the value of that offer by the nearly $20,000 a year it would cost him to get health coverage for his family. Another client discovered that 401(k) contributions could not begin for six months, and still another, spoiled by a generous employer match, discovered that her new 401(k) plan would be worth some $8,000 a year less than her current one. Salary is a critical piece of the compensation package, but it is not the only piece, and clients need to compare all aspects of compensation before commencing the negotiations.

Preparing for the Negotiations

Once Talia has caught her breath and reviewed the full offer, she decides that she would like to negotiate the following points:

Salary

The offer is good, but Talia wants to know if she can do better. I always advise clients to ask for more money, even if they are happy with the salary offered. It's often surprising how much flexibility employers have, and the failure to ask for a better offer means that money gets left on the table

> **Clients should always ask for more money in a salary negotiation.**

Leave

Like many organizations, this one has a basic two-week leave package until someone has been with the company for five years. Talia's current job gives her four weeks of leave, and she doesn't want to lose that important benefit

Telecommuting
		Talia likes to have the ability to work from home, especially when big projects are due, or when the weather is bad. Schedule flexibility is a good thing to clarify during the negotiation process—employers are often much more flexible than they will be in six months. Many clients make the mistake of thinking that they will have more leverage on negotiating a flexible schedule later, after they have "proved themselves." While it's not impossible to negotiate changes to a schedule after starting a job, if you look at Leverage Graph again, you will see that there is minimal leverage to do so.

		Clients may have different priorities—not relocating for a job may be the highest priority, or a flexible schedule may be the most critical issue for a working parent. Title, signing bonuses, profit-sharing, equity stakes, parking privileges, severance packages—these are all the types of things that a client can seek to negotiate as part of the compensation package.

Prioritize Negotiating Items
		Now is the time to determine how to distribute that pile of negotiating leverage the client has been protecting so jealously. There are several ways to prioritize negotiating items—which ones your client chooses will depend on their specific situation.

By Importance

For most clients, the best way to distribute leverage is in order of importance. The client asks about the most important item first, and works their way down to the least critical item. This method ensures that the client brings maximum leverage to bear on the most important issue. In the majority of cases, that issue will be salary, but not always.

By Difficulty

In some cases, clients may want to ask first for the item they think will be most challenging for the employer. For example, if the offer is for a full time position, and the client wants to explore whether the job could be made an 80% time position, asking this question first may make sense. Dropping a request for a part-time position at the end of the salary negotiation is likely to dismay the employer, because it's a big ask, and the employer would be justified in thinking that it should have been raised sooner.

Other issues that may qualify as difficult are start date, if the client wants to delay starting for a significant period of time; job location, where the client would prefer not to relocate to take a job, but do it remotely; and firing authority, if the client senses that a critical early task will be firing current staff.

By "Pocket-ability"

"Pocket-ability" refers to any concession that a client can get simply by asking—no negotiating necessary. These are items that the client can "pocket." Like candy in a bowl, these items can be scooped up quickly and tucked safely in the client's pocket.

> **Consider whether there are items that are free for the asking, and encourage a client to try and "pocket" those items first.**

Issues that can be easily pocketed are those that can be gotten simply by asking a question and receiving a positive response: The client says, "May I have X?" The employer responds, "Yes." The client smiles, tucks the item in her metaphorical "pocket" and moves on to the next item, without having expended any negotiating leverage.

The issue of PTO (paid time off) often has a high "pocket-ability" quotient, and so I usually suggest that clients start off with this issue and see if they can pocket the leave.

To pocket leave, a client might say: "Before we talk about the offer, I have one question. At my last job, I got four weeks of annual leave. I am assuming you'll be able to match that?"

If the employer says "yes", the client pockets the leave and then turns to the offer, all negotiating leverage intact.

Other issues that could be easily pocketed are start date, title, education benefits, reimbursement for professional certifications—anything that can fit into the, "I'm assuming you can…" formula. "I'm assuming that a start date of June 1st will work for you?" or, "I'm assuming that you will cover my annual bar fees and continuing education?"

The great thing about deciding to start with items that can be pocketed is that there is no harm done if the answer is "no" or "I don't know." If the answer is "no", the employer now heads into the negotiation already in the hole—he hasn't been able to meet the candidate's request, disposing him to stretch harder in places where "yes" is more doable. If the answer is, "I don't know", the issue remains open and separate from the rest of the negotiations, so the candidate will have another crack at it.

In prioritizing her list, Talia elects to try and pocket the leave, and then ask about salary, and finally, to probe the employer's willingness to let her telecommute.

Prepare Written Talking Points

The final step in this round is for the client to prepare talking points to use during the negotiation. Most clients find salary negotiations to be extremely stressful, and stress interferes with the ability to remember things. Writing down the points that the client wishes to make, including potential fallback positions, helps to reduce anxiety and insure that nothing is forgotten.

> **Have clients prepare typed talking points to use during salary negotiations.**

Chapter 6: Conducting the Salary Negotiation

With her negotiating goals and priorities clear in her mind, and talking points typed up and sitting in front of her, Talia calls the hiring manager. Let me repeat that. Talia calls the hiring manager.

It is imperative that clients conduct these negotiations in real time—usually over the phone, occasionally face-to-face. Most clients dread the negotiation, and will try to do this via email, or even voice mail. Don't let her do it.

> **Salary negotiations must be done "live."
> No voicemail messages, no emails.**

The negotiating leverage that she so carefully protected all the way through the interview process will dissipate instantly if she just spews all of her negotiating demands in an email or voicemail—the employer will be able to pick and choose which requests to grant. The client may end up with a package that doesn't meet her needs.

Negotiations rest on subtle cues and signals—the speed of a response, the tone of voice. Using email means that the client will be blind to all of this useful information. We can guess, but will never know, how much leverage a client has. If a client is on the phone with an employer, the client will immediately hear if he has pushed too far or too hard, and be able to pull it back. An email that appears too demanding could cost the client the job.

To get your clients on the phone, you are going to have to coach them extensively on what to say, when to say nothing, and what to look and listen for.

Our clients need coaching on what to say during a salary negotiation, but also on what not to say. Just as we coached our clients to leave no gaps during the salary dodge dance, we must now coach them on when to say nothing and let the silence talk.

> **Teach your clients the power of silence.**

Control the Call From The Beginning

When the client calls the employer, it is important to start by saying nice things—about the job or the company or the interview process. Help your client work through the opening remarks. Otherwise, the nervous client is likely to just launch into the negotiations, or, worse yet, let the employer hijack the conversation. The client needs to be in control of the conversation from start to finish, so help figure out how to do it.

Let's see how Talia handles her phone call.

After the complimentary opening—"Good morning. Thank you for giving me the weekend to look over the offer—I appreciate the consideration that you have shown me throughout the interview process."—Talia turns to business. "Do you have a few minutes to talk right now? I'd like to review the offer with you."

The hiring manager indicates that Talia can proceed.

"I had one question before we turn to the offer. At my last position, I was getting four weeks of leave a year. I'm assuming that you will be able to match that?"

As soon as she asks the question, Talia closes her mouth firmly, and waits for the response. Here is where our coaching of clients can be critical. Talia knows how important it is to let the silence stretch. She understands that the silence can tell her all she needs to know.

The hiring manager has been asked a yes-or-no question, so the answer should be pretty quick. The speed of the response will tell Talia the certainty of the answer. If it's a quick "yes," Talia can pocket the leave and move on to negotiating the rest of the package with all of her negotiating leverage intact.

If the answer is a quick "no," there's a high probability that there's no flexibility on the leave issue. If that's a deal-breaker, at least Talia will know where she stands. But if the Talia is still prepared to consider the offer, then she enters the negotiation with a little added leverage—the employer is going to be feeling the pressure to agree to other issues where possible.

If the hiring manager hesitates, it's a good indication that there is some flexibility on the issue. Talia will only get this hint that there's some room to negotiate if she remains quiet. Because here's what is probably going on in the hiring manager's mind while Talia lets the silence stretch: "Hmmm. Can I do that? The company has no firm rules, I'm sure I could get HR to agree. She is coming in at a more senior level, so it seems appropriate. I couldn't live on two weeks leave...I don't want to lose this candidate over some silly bureaucratic rule that I didn't make..."

As Talia waits, the hiring manager realizes that several seconds have passed, and she knows that Talia knows that there is likely some flexibility here. Talia still says nothing. This is incredibly difficult—the urge to say something to break the silence and "rescue" the other person is intense. But the payoff is worth it. Just when Talia thinks she is going to explode from trying to keep her mouth shut, the hiring manager says: "Let me check with HR and see if we can do that for you."

Talia doesn't have an answer yet, but the issue is now in motion, and no negotiating leverage has been used. As an added benefit, the hiring manager is likely to feel some pressure to say, "yes" to something somewhere down the line.

Ask for more money

Having moved the vacation issue down the field, Talia now turns to the offer. She was surprised at how generous the salary offer was, and she doesn't want to push hard on the salary figure. Actually, she'd prefer using her leverage for vacation time and telecommuting. However, she recognizes the importance of asking for more money every time she is faced with a salary negotiation.

> **Clients should ask for more money every time they get a job offer.**

Every client will have to decide how hard she is going to push on the salary question. Some clients are quite pleased with the offer they have received—so pleased that they'd like to skip asking for more money. I encourage every client to ask, because it never hurts. If the answer is "no," nothing is lost, and if the client gets a few thousand bucks more, who can't use the money? Beyond that, many clients are pleasantly surprised to discover that the new employer values them enough to bump the salary, and that starts the job off on a positive note.

For clients who just want to push gently on the salary figure, there are the soft approaches:

"Do you have any flexibility on the salary?"

"Can you do better on the salary number?"

"On the salary figure, is that the maximum you can offer?"

Vocal tone is important—the questions should be asked without an edge, in a conversational tone. But once the question is asked, the client needs to remain quiet. It is so tempting for clients to add, "But it's ok if you can't, I'm very happy with the offer." Poof—negotiating leverage all gone. Have your client practice asking the question and then not saying anything else for 30 seconds to help get comfortable with silence.

> **Have your clients practice sitting quietly—and time them.**

For other clients, the salary figure is disappointing, to say the least. For these offers, a big push is needed. Here is where the research into salary ranges that you coached your client to do all those weeks ago will come to the rescue. When an offer is unacceptably low, here are some approaches for clients to try:

"On the salary offer: Based on my research, the salary range for this position is $75,000 to $125,000. Since I have a number of years of experience in these types of positions, and have direct experience with your customer population, I thought that I would come in close to the top of the range." Then wait for the response. Remember, the longer the silence, the more likely that there is some debate going on in the hiring manager's mind.

"I was somewhat disappointed with the salary number. Based on my experience and salary history, I was hoping for $65,000." Stop. See if the employer agrees to the figure. If the employer indicates that he can't do that, then ask the follow-up question: "How close can you get me to that figure?"

"I'm sorry, I can't accept the position at this salary. Do you have any flexibility?" or, "Can you get me to (number)?" This approach is only used if the salary is a deal-breaker and the client is prepared to walk away from the job. But if the client is clear that they will not take the position at the salary offered, this is how to use that leverage:

"That salary is on the low side. Would you be prepared to make this a 32 hour position?" This is an interesting counter, and isn't right for every client, but for clients who don't need the money, and would be willing to work for less money in exchange for a shorter work week, this can be a good fallback. And it can work. Many organizations don't have the budgets, but they have the scheduling flexibility. If a client is interested in part-time work, this can be an acceptable solution for both sides.

The most important thing about these approaches is that they indicate that the employer needs to do more than toss a couple of thousand bucks into the pot. The gambit may not be successful, but at least the client knows exactly how high the employer is prepared to go.

For some clients, deciding to take the lower number is a tough decision—they need the job, but the pay cut is hard to swallow. Your client is allowed to thank the employer for the information, and to ask for a little more time to think: "I appreciate your taking the time to talk to me about the offer. I continue to be interested in the job; I just need to do a bit more thinking about whether I can take something at this salary level. Can I run some numbers and speak with my partner and get back to you tomorrow?"

It is important for clients to know that they can hang onto a job offer while negotiating hard for a better deal. Notice that in the formulation above, the client has kept a firm grip on the offer, has not issued any ultimatums, and has allowed themselves the ability to come back with either another counter offer, an acceptance of the offer, or a well-justified refusal of the offer.

Sometimes, just asking for time to think will encourage the employer to rummage around and find something else to offer. One of my clients was disappointed with a salary figure. The employer offered to start tuition benefits immediately. Since the client was beginning an MBA program that fall, this constituted a significant increase in the compensation package. Everyone was happy.

Talia doesn't need to make a big push, so here's what she says next:

"I have a couple of questions about the offer. On the salary figure, do you have any flexibility?

She waits, and the employer hesitates for a moment, then reveals they could probably round the offer up another $2500. Talia accepts that with an expression of gratitude.

Now comes the most important thing on Talia's list—telecommuting. She has done an excellent job of husbanding her negotiating leverage to use on this point. This item is important to her—the right answer will turn this from a good job into a great job. Talia decides to level with the employer.

"I am very interested in this company, and I think I can get up to speed quickly. I know that I work most efficiently when I can have large blocks of time to focus on my work. If I could have the flexibility to work from home, this would truly be a dream job. Are you able to make this a telecommuting position?"

Talia's pitched it hard, but she hasn't given an ultimatum—"Do this or I don't take the job." She can still decide to take the job, even if the employer denies her request.

The employer doesn't say "yes" or "no" right away, but expresses concern about Talia bonding with the group, and about how to manage the work of an employee that he can't see. Talia acknowledges the concerns, and inquires about alternatives—being on-site for the first month, then slowly phasing in the telecommuting, working with her boss to establish clear metrics that will let him know she is doing her job. By the end of the discussion, they have an agreement to phase-in the telecommuting over a 90 day period, and Talia has agreed to be in the office for certain regular meetings and events.

All of our clients have the capacity to manage a salary negotiation the way that Talia has. What makes it so challenging is the emotional component. Clients have to be able to master their anxiety and their fears repeatedly during this process. In my experience, clients who have been coached intensively on what they are trying to accomplish, and the techniques to use at each stage of the process, allows them to better tolerate the anxiety of the process and achieve a positive result.

> **Extensive and explicit coaching on techniques and tactics can help clients manage the intense anxiety of salary negotiations.**

Get it in Writing

Every single salary offer needs to be committed to writing. It doesn't need to be a fancy letter—a simple exchange of emails confirming the details of the offer will suffice—but it must be done. I can't tell you how many clients have discovered that a boss mis-remembers a salary deal, or another detail of the agreement, and how many more clients have started work only to find that the person that they negotiated the deal with has been fired or has moved to another position. Most organizations will honor deals that are written down, so make sure your clients get their hard-won salary packages in writing.

They'll need coaching on this, too, because sometimes employers balk. I encourage clients to be proactive, by bringing up the written agreement as soon as an offer is concluded: "Thank you so much for your flexibility on these issues. I am so excited to be joining this organization. Now, are you going to put all this in an offer letter, or would you prefer that I draft an email on what we agreed to and then you can either agree to it or modify the language to reflect your understanding?"

If the employer resists putting the offer in written form, counsel your client to persist: "I know I am being a bit picky, and it's not because I think anything will happen here. It's just that I've seen what trouble can be caused when things aren't in writing, so I have learned that even though it's uncomfortable, it's important to get the elements of the offer written down."

In Talia's case, she's still waiting to hear back on vacation time, so she says: "This is all great. We just need to hear back from HR on the leave issue. Assuming they approve the four weeks of annual leave, will you send me a letter with all the details of the offer?"

Accept the Offer

Now is the time for the client to be fulsome with her praise about the company, her new boss, and the HR department, anyone who was involved. If anyone felt a bit pushed during the negotiations, now is the time to smooth any potentially ruffled feathers with generous thanks for the company's flexibility, its professional approach, whatever is worthy of note. Clients who negotiate offers like this have likely pushed the employer harder than they are accustomed to, so it makes sense to express gratitude for all of the concessions that have been made, big and small. It's easy to be magnanimous in victory.

Defining Success in Salary Negotiations

There's an interesting side effect to all of this intensive coaching on salary negotiations. After going through all of this coaching and successfully getting much of what they decided to ask for, clients sometimes express a sense of failure because they didn't get everything they asked for. They have gotten so excited about their newfound ability to negotiate, they are disappointed when they discover the limits of what their leverage can get them.

> **Success in a salary negotiation means eventually getting to "no."**

I remind my clients that in order to ensure that you get everything that's on the table, you actually have to ask for MORE than the employer is willing to give. It is only when the employer says "Sorry, can't quite manage that," that the client knows that they have gotten the best possible deal from the negotiation. So the fact that the client didn't get everything asked for in the negotiation indicates success. The client used their leverage to its best advantage and got everything possible. For many of our clients not used to the world of negotiations it doesn't seem right to define success as getting turned down.

So make sure that the client understands that the goal of the salary negotiation process is to discover all the places where the employer has flexibility to improve the offer. When an employer finally says "no," the negotiation is complete.

Negotiations are a game. Neither side has full information on what the other side wants and needs, so both sides go through a series of maneuvers to obtain more information and increase leverage. Our job as career coaches and counselors is to help our clients understand the rules of the game. Some clients will be more comfortable with this game than others, but even if clients limit their negotiating to asking for more money, this will be an important addition to their career toolbox. And with proper coaching, many of them will discover that they can be very effective advocates on their own behalf.

Chapter 7: Negotiating Other Workplace Issues

With modifications, everything that you have taught your clients about salary negotiations can be applied to other types of workplace negotiations. Promotions, raises, bonuses, schedule changes and exit packages are the most common negotiations that clients will have to manage at work.

The game is the same. The biggest mistake clients make in workplace negotiations is not going through all of the steps, from assessing leverage, through the early preparations and information-gathering to setting up the final negotiating session. So let's walk through the process of negotiating a workplace issue.

The Negotiating Process for Workplace Negotiations

Find Leverage on the Job

We started salary negotiations with the Chopra Leverage Graph, and it remains the starting point for understanding how much leverage a client has. Once an offer has been accepted, the client's leverage decreases, but it does not return to zero. Most clients still possess some leverage—the trick is to find it. Here are some things that may indicate that leverage exists:

—A client who has had a stellar year has increased leverage. Most employers want to keep star performers and are likely to grant what is being requested.

—Longevity can confer leverage, especially if the company doesn't have redundancy of the client's skill set, or if the client has developed a strong set of relationships with vendors or customers. Once an employer has paid to move someone up a learning curve, it has some incentive not to go back to the beginning again.

—Personal power should never be overlooked. Some clients will be well-liked and respected in their organizations. Supervisors will want to make them happy, and that constitutes leverage.

—Critical events or projects can generate leverage. If a client is deeply involved in a critical organizational function, the company has an interest in keeping the employee.

—Timing of negotiations can affect how much leverage exists. Clients will usually have more leverage for getting a raise during the annual review process. Employers have set aside time and money to assess and reward performance. Asking for a raise mid-cycle is usually a tough sell. But leverage in asking for a bonus may be highest right after a key win—an important new client or contract, for example.

—Information can be a critical component of negotiating leverage. I encourage all of my clients to have a good internal intelligence network, precisely because information is power. If a client knows that the company is struggling to find a certain skill set, then the client has some confidence that a raise request, or a request to telecommute, will be treated with consideration.

—Rising stars have leverage. If the client is getting lots of plum assignments and face-time with senior management, that's a good sign that there is some leverage to make a request. If a client knows that an assignment has been languishing, undone, in his inbox, that may be a good indication that there will be some resistance to his request for more responsibility. That doesn't mean he can't ask, it just means that he needs to be prepared for the questions and concerns that a boss is likely to raise, and have convincing and truthful responses.

Gather Information and Intelligence
Just as our clients were coached to collect salary data in the run-up to a salary negotiation, they need to be coached to assemble data relevant to the current workplace negotiation:

—Salary discussions require that the client assemble a dossier detailing highlights of the past year's performance, including a nice pile of complimentary emails from clients and co-workers, if available.

—Discussions of flextime or telecommuting should be preceded by extensive research into the company's existing policy, as well as conversations with anyone in the company who already has the desired flexibility.

—Negotiation of an exit package should not commence until the client has reviewed the company's employee handbook, consulted a lawyer, and talked to anyone else who may have been recently severed from the company.

Clients tend to focus on what they want. The goal of this round of information-gathering is to figure out what the boss is going to want to know, and be ready to answer the questions. It also helps the client design the request in a way that is most likely to be accepted. If Maurice wants to take time off when his child is born, and the company gives women six weeks of maternity leave, he is likely to be successful if he requests six weeks of leave, and may have a much harder time requesting additional leave.

Prepare for the Negotiation

In interview and salary negotiations, the focus is on preparing clients to respond and dodge questions about salary and compensation. Workplace negotiations require clients to prepare just as intensively for the types of questions they are likely to get.

Clients should list every possible question or objection the boss might make to the planned request, and prepare a short, credible response. If the client is the first one in the department to try working part-time, or working from home, the client can expect lots of questions about how the boss would handle such requests from others. The client doesn't have to be able to solve the problem, just be prepared to offer some constructive thoughts.

In interview negotiations, the client wanted to redirect the conversation away from the topic of salary. In most other workplace negotiations, the goal is to keep the conversation going. As long as the boss is asking questions, he hasn't said "no."

This is also the time for the client to decide what possible fallback positions exist, if the client doesn't get their first choice. If June wants to work from home five days a week, will she accept three days as a fallback? If Tony wants to work 35 hours a week while he attends graduate school, is he willing to work longer hours the week of the annual conference? If Maya wants to change her hours to come in at 7:30 a.m. instead of 9:00 a.m., is she prepared to be flexible to cover a co-worker's planned vacation?

Clients need to be ready with acceptable fallback positions, because if they aren't, the boss may propose an unacceptable alternative, and the client won't have a quick response. A negotiation is like a game of chess, so encourage clients to review all possible moves before they start the negotiation.

Conduct All Workplace Negotiations In Person

Having reviewed their leverage position and prepared for all possible questions and objections, your client is now ready to make the pitch. This should always be done face-to-face: just as with salary negotiations, the speed of responses and the body language will supply as much information as what the boss is saying. If a client emails a boss with a request, the boss has time to formulate objections, making it more likely that the boss will say "no."

In almost all cases, it is best to schedule time to speak with the boss. This ensures that time has been set aside to focus on the request. Asking for something that requires the boss to commit time and resources to making it happen is not something that should be done in the hallway or via a head-poke into the boss' office. In general, a surprised boss is a grouchy boss, and that's usually not a good way to begin a negotiation.

Clients are sometimes reluctant to schedule time, fearing that the request will simply trigger the conversation before the client is ready. This is when email, voicemail and meeting request software can help. The client can request a meeting with a generic, "I'd like a few minutes to talk when you have a chance. I have some questions about my position." That's true enough, but vague enough, that the boss is likely to be curious, and schedule the meeting. If the boss asks for more information, the client can simply reply that it's something better handled in person.

Once the meeting starts, the client wants to keep the conversation moving smoothly, and ideally, wants to keep it low-key and friendly. The more agitated someone is, the less likely they are to be able to assess the pros and cons of the situation. A boss who is angry or worried, is more likely to shut down the conversation with an instant, "no way," than a boss who is relaxed and calm.

Even when negotiating an exit package, which is likely to occur within the context of strained relations, it is vital for the client to stay calm and non-defensive. The ability to stay focused on the negotiation and not get drawn into an emotional tit-for-tat is a way to increase leverage—the one who is most calm and focused usually wins.

The client requested the meeting, so just as with salary negotiations, the client will start the conversation. The client will deliver their prepared pitch for whatever it is they are seeking and then stop and wait for the boss' reaction. Encourage your clients to sit quietly and listen until the boss has completed their response. Ideally, the client wants to know all the objections to a proposal before framing a response.

In an ideal world, your client has come back to you for additional coaching on this workplace negotiation, because they will need help thinking through how to respond to objections and concerns from the boss. The instinctive reaction is to defend their position. The better response, initially, is for the client to restate what the boss has said and ask questions: "You are concerned that a change in my work hours means that I won't be in the office when the weekly report is due. If we worked out a system for my handling the weekly report that guarantees you the type of coverage you want, would that help?"

> **Prepare clients to address concerns non-defensively, with a question and not an argument.**

Using questions to probe for flexibility in the boss' negotiating position is exactly what the client did during salary negotiations.

Encourage your clients to use their personal power in these situations, especially if they know they are liked and respected by their colleagues and supervisors. Many clients discount how much they are valued within an organization. Sometimes a statement such as: "This is really important to me. I love my job, but I need more schedule flexibility. What can we do to achieve that?" will do more to encourage flexibility than the best power-point presentation of facts on why flexible schedules improve worker productivity.

Get it in Writing

Any agreement reached needs to be put in writing. An email exchange summarizing the agreement is sufficient. This is particularly important for workplace negotiations because it is easy for one party to think this is a done deal, while the other thinks this is something to think about. Putting the agreement into written form helps both sides be clear on what was agreed to, and often ensures the success of the endeavor.

Defining Success, Dealing with Failure

Help clients decide ahead of time what constitutes an acceptable outcome. With schedule issues, there are often multiple outcomes that the client can live with. In the case of a bonus, there is probably a range of compensation that will feel like "enough." But when it comes to requesting a promotion or a raise, success is often defined by a simple "yes" or "no." The client needs to decide up front what will be acceptable.

If the negotiation fails to achieve the client's objectives, and it does happen, then the client needs to be prepared to end the negotiation on their own terms. If a raise or promotion is requested, and is denied, clients are often tempted to issue ultimatums or threaten to quit. My advice is to find a different, but still powerful way to end the negotiation.

Threatening to quit means that the client has to go find a new job, fairly quickly, or they will be revealed to have been bluffing, which will damage their reputation and credibility for as long as they remain with the company, and, depending on the field, even after they leave.

It is far better to sit quietly for a moment, then look straight at the boss and say: "That's good to know, thank-you." And then walk out. It's an ambiguous ending, and it is meant to be. The client hasn't said what they are going to do and has given themselves time to weigh their options carefully.

> **Client's don't have to quit a job just because a negotiation failed.**

Some clients, once they have considered their options, do end up deciding to stay, even if they don't get the raise that they requested, and that is OK. Perhaps the boss' "no" was the inspiration the client needed to launch their own business. But since that takes time, the client wants to stay on the payroll for a year or so. Or maybe the client wants to go back to school, and it's easier to do that from the current job. Or perhaps the client is determined not to jump until they find the perfect position That may take a while.

Just because a client asked for something and failed to get it does not mean they have to quit their job. Make sure your clients are prepped so they don't quit their job in a fit of pique.

Conclusion

Our great gift to our clients is not the fabulous new job that they get after working with us, although that makes all of us feel good. Our great gift is the training in workplace skills that will continue to pay dividends across the client's career. Most people lack the necessary skills to negotiate effectively, whether for salary and compensation or some other workplace objective, not because it is hard, but because negotiations are done so rarely. When you coach your clients to become effective negotiators on their own behalf, you have given them something of lasting value, and they will consider the time spent working with you to have been worth every penny they invested in the process.

Acknowledgements

Even a slim volume such as this one owes a large debt of gratitude to all who helped to nurture it along the way.

Cindy Barrilleaux, (WriteYourBest.com) served as the midwife for this and all my writing endeavors, convincing me that I could, if I just pushed hard enough, get it done.

This project—a guide to coaching salary negotiations--was originally suggested by Wendy Enelow (www.CareerThoughtleaders.com).

Sylvia Tooker (www.BearData.com) is responsible for all things related to my website, including the links to buy this book.

Mindy Reed (www.authorsassistant.com) and her team who wrangled this project from manuscript to published book.

Anne Grey has provided the safe place for me to wrestle with issues professional and personal. I owe my career as a counselor to Lea Sloan, who all those years ago suggested that change was possible and then helped me make it.

My colleagues and supervisors at the U.S. Department of Commerce and the Office of the U.S. Trade Representative were my mentors and tutors in the ways of negotiation.

Finally, none of this would have been possible without my husband, Ajai, who has never wavered in his love or his support, and our son, Neil, who infuses each day with joy.

Made in the USA
Middletown, DE
03 January 2015